Thailand small**Hotels**

Thailand small Hotels | Hua Hin, Cha-am and Pranburi

Copyright © 2011 Li- Zenn Publishing Limited

Published in Asia in 2011 by
Page One Publishing Pte Ltd
20 Kaki Bukit View
Kaki Bukit Techpark II
Singapore 415956
Tel: [65] 6742-2088
Fax: [65] 6744-2088
enquiries@pageonegroup.com
www.pageonegroup.com

First published 2011 by Li-Zenn Publishing Limited
81 Sukhumvit 26 Bangkok 10110 Thailand
T: +66 (0) 2259 2096, F: +66 (0) 2661 2017
li-zenn@li-zenn.com, www.li-zenn.com

ISBN of Li-Zenn Edition
ISBN 978-616-7191-28-7

| | | |
|---|---|---|
| **Publisher** | : | Nithi Sthapitanonda |
| **Managing Director** | : | Suluck Visavapattamawon |
| **Deputy Managing Director** | : | Pisut Lertdumrikarn |
| | | Kiattisak Veteewootacharn |
| **Distributor** | | |
| **Thailand** | : | Li-Zenn Books Limited |
| | | 81 Sukhumvit 26 Bangkok 10110 Thailand |
| | | T: +66 (0) 2259 2096, F: +66 (0) 2661 2017 |
| | | li-zenn@li-zenn.com, www.li-zenn.com |
| **International** | : | Page One Publishing Pte Ltd |
| | | 20 Kaki Bukit View Techpark II Singapore 415956 |
| | | T: +(65) 6742 2088, F: +(65) 6744 2088 |
| | | www.pageonegroup.com |
| **Printer** | : | Dami Editorial & Printing Services Co.Ltd. |
| **Front cover** | : | AKA Resort Hua Hin, Hua Hin |
| **Back cover** | : | Baan Bayan Beach Hotel, Hua Hin |
| | | Yaiya Resort, Cha-am |
| | | Let's Sea Hua Hin Al Fresco Resort, Hua Hin |
| | | Villa Maroc Resort, Pranburi |
| | | The Hen Hua Hin, Hua Hin |

**Hotel images sketch by** Sasi Veerasethakul

ISBN 978-981-428-628-2

Printed in China

THAILAND
# smallHotels
# Hua Hin
## Cha-am and Pranburi

PAGE ONE

# Introduction

Bangkok

1

2    Gulf of Thailand

1 Phetchaburi
2 Prachuap Khiri Khan

The upper southern region of Thailand is comprised of three famous coastal holiday districts located along the Gulf of Thailand namely, Hua Hin, Pranburi, and Cha-am. The province of Prachuap Khiri Khan hosts Hua Hin and Pranburi, while Phetchaburi boasts Cha-am as its famous beach resort.

In the past, Hua Hin was recognized among Thais as a holiday sanctuary for the aristocracy seeking an escape from Bangkok's summer heat. The name Hua Hin was prompted by area's topography, which is made up of rows of stone hillocks lying along the fine beach. With a growing reputation, Hua Hin became even better known with the opening of the southern railway line and its associated infrastructure, which was followed by a 5-star hotel and a golf course. The prosperity of the area then peaked when the King Prajadhipok, Rama VII, commissioned the construction of a summer palace, which he named 'Wang Klai Kangwon'. As a result, members of the royal family and other nobles increasingly spent time at Hua Hin, building their own holiday homes there. Today, Hua Hin is a renowned destination among tourists for its white sand, serene beach atmosphere, and safe swimming conditions. It is also only a short distance from Bangkok and is easily reached by road, rail, or air.

When people started looking for a new holiday retreat, Cha-am, a small fishing village nearby Hua Hin, was developed as a tourist destination. One of the distinctive features that helped open up the city to tourism

was the inshore street where there was accommodation for middle-class travellers, as well as foreigners. In consequence, the reputation of Hua Hin and Cha-am as holiday destinations spread out around the world. Nowadays, the pattern of tourism is changing in order to cater to travellers' varying tastes and preferences, and accordingly new beaches close to Hua Hin, such as Pranburi, Kui Buri, Sam Roi Yot and Thap Sakae, are increasingly winning the attention of holidaymakers, and city plans have been designed and developed rapidly to turn these beach locales into alternative vacation choices. As a result, the tourism industry has blossomed and generated enormous income for both the local communities and the country as a whole. Hotels and resorts situated either right on the beach or inshore at Hua Hin, Cha-am, and Pranburi are generally of just two or three storeys and with a small number of guestrooms, or otherwise bungalows and villas, while the style of architecture and interior design is variously Modern, Tropical, Boutique, Contemporary, or Country.

However, some accommodations preserve their identity by retaining the original Hua Hin, or Colonial, architectural style. The style is well expressed by semi-wooden structures, steep roofs suitable for the Thai climate, and colour schemes that imitate the natural environment, such as yellow from the golden shower tree, orange from the flame tree, and azure from the sea. Despite the various styles of architecture and design, the hotels and resorts in Hua Hin, Cha-am, and Pranburi strive to maintain a holiday culture that is well-praised by many tourism authorities for having high standards of service and management. More importantly, the charm of local hospitality reflects a love of history, culture, and tradition that is not swayed by the changing influences of marketing and globalization.

The book, Thailand smallHotels: Hua Hin, Cha-am and Pranburi, is part of a series that informs readers about small hotels where guestrooms do not number more than 60, and also where importance is given to architectural style interior and landscape design. Believing that the philosophy of being 'small' is able to create an intimate atmosphere and be in touch with the beauty hidden in the comfort and convenience of the accommodation. Furthermore, visitors will also experience the sensual art of local living to fulfill their holiday dreams to perfection.

# Contents

Cha-am

Hua Hin

Pranburi

Sam Roi Yot

Kui Buri

Thap Sakae

1 Phetchaburi
2 Prachuap Khiri Khan

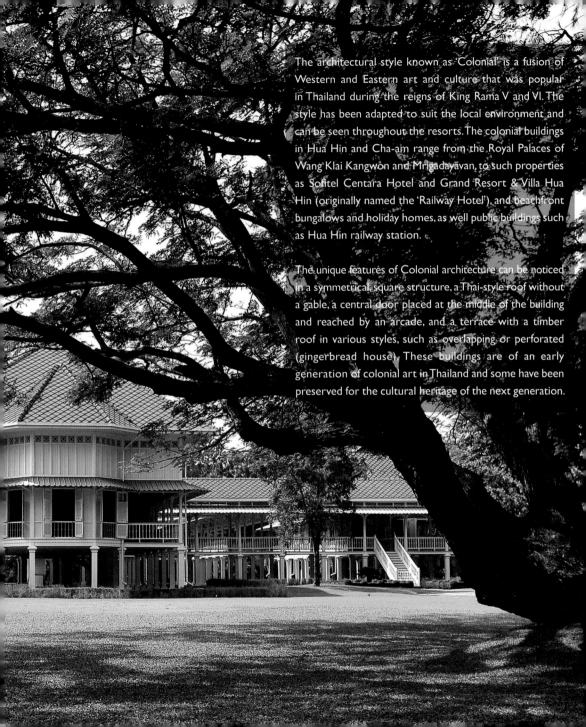

The architectural style known as 'Colonial' is a fusion of Western and Eastern art and culture that was popular in Thailand during the reigns of King Rama V and VI. The style has been adapted to suit the local environment and can be seen throughout the resorts. The colonial buildings in Hua Hin and Cha-am range from the Royal Palaces of Wang Klai Kangwon and Mrigadayavan, to such properties as Sofitel Centara Hotel and Grand Resort & Villa Hua Hin (originally named the 'Railway Hotel'), and beachfront bungalows and holiday homes, as well public buildings such as Hua Hin railway station.

The unique features of Colonial architecture can be noticed in a symmetrical, square structure, a Thai-style roof without a gable, a central door placed at the middle of the building and reached by an arcade, and a terrace with a timber roof in various styles, such as overlapping or perforated (gingerbread house). These buildings are of an early generation of colonial art in Thailand and some have been preserved for the cultural heritage of the next generation.

# Cha-am

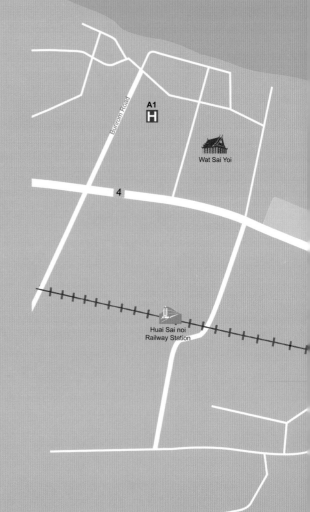

| | | | |
|---|---|---|---|
| ✈ | Airport | 🛒 | Market |
| ★ | Important Place | ✚ | Hospital |
| 🏛 | City Hall | 🚌 | Bus Station |
| 🛕 | Temple | ✝ | Church |
| ⛰ | Mountain | 🐘 | Elephant Camp |
| 🚉 | Railway Station | 💧 | Waterfall |
| 🛡 | Police Station | **1** | Road Number |

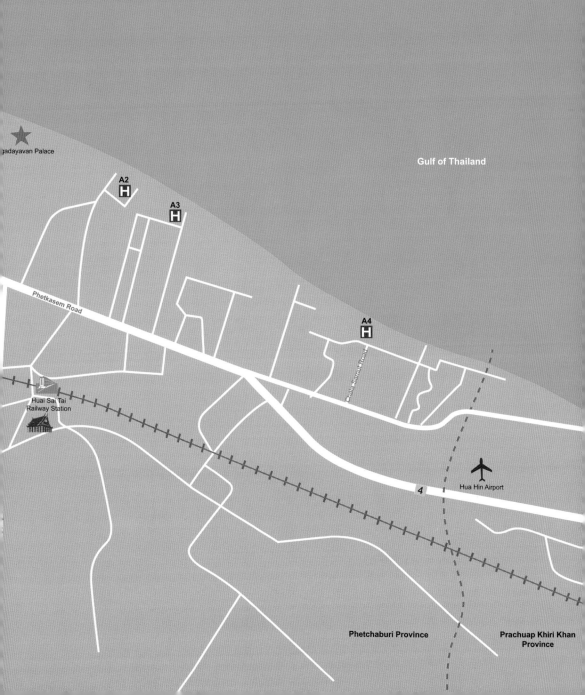

Gulf of Thailand

ฺadayavan Palace

**A2**

**A3**

**A4**

Phetkasem Road

Chule Samut Road

Huai Sai Tai
Railway Station

4

Hua Hin Airport

Phetchaburi Province

Prachuap Khiri Khan
Province

# Cher Resort

เฌอ รีสอร์ท

**Type:** Boutique Hotel
**Style:** Contemporary
**Room type:** 36 Rooms; 2 Sky Jacuzzi Beach Front Villa Rooms, 8 Blissfully Green Villa Rooms,
6 The Pool Paradise Rooms, 6 The Sea Spirit Rooms, 14 Panoramic Sea view Rooms
**Room rate:** 4,000 to 16,000 THB
**Facilities:** Pool, Restaurant, Bar, Library
**Architect and Landscape Architect:** Piyachanok Wijarn

Cher resort is a tropical getaway located between Cha-am and Hua Hin, on the northwest coast of the Gulf of Thailand. This luxurious beachside property is designed as a 'Modern-Nature' destination that is so hip, chic and cool that you leave vowing to come back soon. Each room provides something different in a choice of delights, such as a 3-metre-high sky Jacuzzi, a two-person-size outdoor bathtub, or a salt-water heated pool. Every creative aspect of the space has been meticulously thought out, selected and presented to give you the best holiday experience.

'Cher' in Thai means 'tree'. In keeping with the name, the main color scheme is earth and monotone, while a variety of surrounding trees and the landscaped gardens give both shade and a fresh, breezy atmosphere, allowing you to surrender to the charms of nature. Also distinctive are the stylish buffalo figures scattered around the resort, a reflection on its former name of Bang Kwai, 'Buffalo Village'

**Address**
924, Bureerom Road, Cha-am, Phetchaburi, 76120
**T:** +66 (0) 3250 8508-9, **F:** +66 (0) 3250 8507, **E:** rsvn@cherresort.com
www.cherresort.com

# Yaiya Resort
ยายย่า รีสอร์ท

**Type:** Boutique Hotel
**Style:** Tropical Modern
**Room type:** 40 Units; Three-bedroom Yaiya Pavilion 1 Unit,
Two-bedroom SaSala Pool Villa 2 Units, One-bedroom SaSala Pool Villa 8 Units,
Suite Sea Terrace 6 Units, Deluxe Sea Terrace 15 Units, Deluxe Terrace 8 Units
**Room rate:** start from 5,000 THB
**Facilities:** Pool, Spa, Restaurant, Lounge, Bar, Library
**Architect and Interior Architect:** Habita
**Landscape Architect:** Insideout

The Thai term 'taak arkas', meaning 'to be exposed to the breeze', is how Thais once typically described their summer holidays. With the invention of air-conditioning, this habit has been largely forgotten, but Yaiya Resort aims to restore the traditional ambience.

Designed over two storeys and each with a pool, the villas at Yaiya comprise a living sala (Thai pavilion) and sun deck on the upper floor to catch the cool breeze, while on the lower level are air-conditioned bedroom and bathroom set within a walled garden, the main prerequisite for tropical living. There is also a block of individual guestrooms featuring deep verandahs facing the sea. Rather than copying traditional Thai architecture, the design of both the villas and the guestroom block is stylishly modern, simple and unpretentious, highlighted by local touches.

The pool villas are grouped together and positioned so that the pool faces the garden, while the main building takes advantage of a deeper contour change by incorporating parking space below and a guest arrival area on the upper court level. The landscaped site follows the gentle slope of the natural terrain and is simply but pleasantly laid out with lawn, trees and shrubs.

Facilities at the Beach Club consist of pool, restaurant, bar and spa. Simple and rustic is the predominant theme, and al fresco dining is emphasized.

**Address**
1390/19, Phetkasem Road, Cha-am, Phetchaburi, 76120
**T:** +66 (0) 3240 6111, **F:** +66 (0) 3240 6117, **E:** contact@yaiyaresort.com
www.yaiyaresort.com

# Devasom Hua Hin Resort

เทวาศรม หัวหิน รีสอร์ท

**Type:** Boutique Hotel
**Style:** Vintage Hua Hin
**Room type:** 14 Rooms and 10 Villas; 8 Seaside Deluxe Rooms,
6 Seaside Suite Rooms, 8 Beach Villas, 2 Beachfront Villas
**Room rate:** 5,200 to 10,600 THB
**Facilities:** Pool, Spa, Restaurant, Lounge, Library
**Architect and Landscape Architect:** Saran Soontornsuk
**Interior Architect:** Virat Limsuansub

At Devasom guests are invited to unwind, forget time and simply relax. Delicately developed to bring back the enchanting beauty of olden times, the resort offers a glamorous vacation experience, with all elements designed to convey a contemporary interpretation of Hua Hin's classic charm.

Inspired by Hua Hin's seaside glamour of the past, Devasom features rooms and villas crafted in old colonial style and with balconies offering unsurpassed sea views. Each villa also features either a private terrace and garden, or an adjoining family deck. Directly next to the beach is a large horizon-edge swimming pool with Jacuzzi.

Devasom Hua Hin Resort won the 'Thailand Boutique Awards 2010', supported by the Tourism Authority of Thailand, in the Culture Category for the southern region, which gave recognition to its conservation of a historical lifestyle in its architecture, interior design, and environment.

**Address**
1446 / 23, Phetkasem Road (km 221.5), Phetchaburi, 76120
**T:** +66 (0) 3244 2789, **F:** +66 (0) 3244 2795, **E:** reservation@devasom.com
www.devasom.com

# The Haven Resort Hua Hin

เดอะ ฮาเว่น รีสอร์ท หัวหิน

**Type:** Boutique Hotel
**Style:** Contemporary
**Room type:** 46 Rooms and 7 Villas; 18 Superior Rooms, 28 Deluxe Rooms,
3 Villas, Villas @ Sea 2 Units, 1 Suite, Suite @ Sea 1 Unit
**Room rate:** 7,700 to 21,200 THB
**Facilities:** Pool, Spa, Restaurant, Lounge, Bar, Fitness

At Haven, rooms and nature are harmoniously united. The idea is exquisitely reflected in the stylish simplicity of the layout, with a long passage leading to the beach and the centre of the resort where an infinity-edge pool seems to merge with the sea. Indeed, here is luxury amidst scenic nature. Moreover, the design emphasizes privacy while at same time allowing everyone to fully indulge in the charming landscape. All guestrooms and villas are decorated with local handicrafts made of natural materials, which provides a pleasingly cozy atmosphere.

You can immerse yourself in a blissful relaxing atmosphere at the open Moon Desk on the top of each villa, enjoying the peaceful ambience while laying back to read a book or listen to the whisper of sleepless waves. Whether savouring the sunshine or relishing the light of a silvery moon, you'll experience a memorable destination where your total satisfaction is all that matters. Truly a haven.

**Address**
1449, Chala Samut Road, Cha-am, Phetchaburi, 76120
**T:** +66 (0) 3252 3023, **F:** +66 (0) 3252 3028, **E:** sales@haven-huahin.com
www.haven-huahin.com

As for beach activities, when visiting Hua Hin the image of horse riding along the beach is a memorable one that has been around for 40 years. Visitors are able to enjoy not only beachfront sightseeing but also the beauty of classic architecture and the changing face of Hua Hin.

Another popular activity for all Buddhists is to make merit by offering food to monks who walk along the beach early in the morning. People also have the chance to experience breezy cool weather and listen to the sound of calm waves while watching the first light of day at the edge of the long white sandy beach. Another 'must do' that most foreign travellers like to experience while staying in Hua Hin, Cha-am and Pranburi is to pamper oneself with a spa treatment and massage session to reduce body and mind tension.

# Northern and
# Central Hua Hin

Gulf of Thailand

| | | |
|---|---|---|
| H | **B1** | Rest Detail Hotel Hua Hin |
| H | **B2** | Piman Plearnwan |
| H | **B3** | The Herbs by the Sea Hotel and Spa |
| H | **B4** | Dune Hua Hin Hotel |
| H | **B5** | The Hen Hua Hin |
| H | **B6** | Putahracsa Hua Hin |
| H | **B7** | Baan Laksasubha Resort Hua Hin |
| H | **B8** | Baan Bayan Beach Hotel |
| H | **B9** | AKA Resort Guti Hua Hin, |
| | | AKA Resort Hua Hin |

B1
Klai Kangwon Palace
Wat Klai Kangwon
Soi 19
Soi 21
Soi 31
Soi 33
Soi 35
To Cha-am
Golden Place Supermarket
4
B2
Hua Hin Hospital

| | | | |
|---|---|---|---|
| ✈ | Airport | 🏪 | Market |
| ★ | Important Place | ✚ | Hospital |
| 🏛 | City Hall | 🚌 | Bus Station |
| 🛕 | Temple | † | Church |
| ⛰ | Mountain | 🐘 | Elephant Camp |
| 🚉 | Railway Station | 🔱 | Waterfall |
| 🛡 | Police Station | **1** | Road Number |

Khao Noi
Wat Khao Iti Sukt
To Pala-U Waterfall

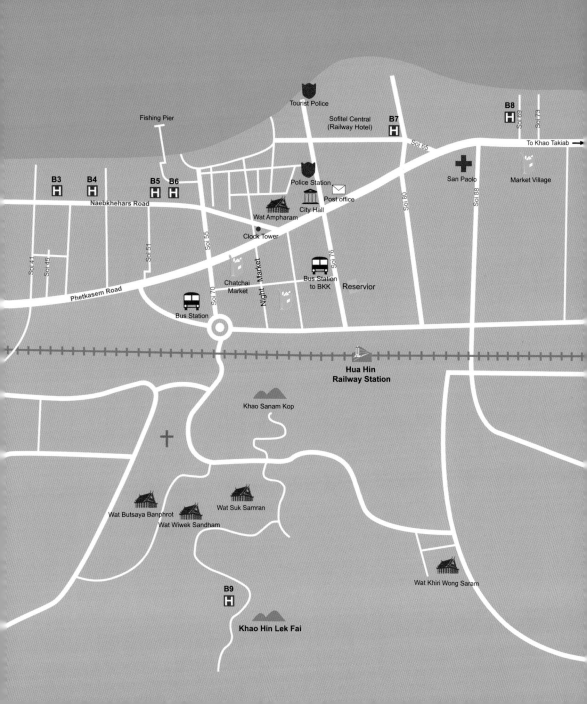

Fishing Pier

Tourist Police

Sofitel Central
(Railway Hotel)

**B7**
H

**B8**
H

Sol 69
Sol 73

To Khao Takiab →

Sol 66

**B3**
H

**B4**
H

**B5**
H

**B6**
H

Naebkhehars Road

Police Station

Wat Ampharam

Post office

City Hall

San Paolo

Market Village

Sol 80

Sol 88

Sol 51

Sol 55

Clock Tower

Sol 76

Phetkasem Road

Soi 41

Soi 45

Chatchai
Market

Night Market

Bus Station
to BKK

Reservior

Bus Station

Soi 70

Hua Hin
Railway Station

Khao Sanam Kop

Wat Butsaya Banphrot

Wat Wiwek Sandham

Wat Suk Samran

Wat Khiri Wong Saram

**B9**
H

**Khao Hin Lek Fai**

# Rest Detail Hotel Hua Hin

โรงแรมเรสดีเทล โฮเทล หัวหิน

**Type:** Boutique Resort
**Style:** Modern Oriental
**Room type:** 52 Rooms and 4 Pavilions; 14 Rest Green Rooms, 10 Rest Spirit Rooms,
10 Rest Horizon Rooms, 12 Pool Village Rooms, 4 Beach Village Rooms, 1 North Rest Pavilion,
1 South Rest Pavilion, 1 Beach Rest Pavilion, 1 Grand Rest Pavilion
**Room rate:** 8,000++ to 10,000++ THB
**Facilities:** Pool, Spa, Restaurant, Bar
**Architect:** Trend Design
**Interior Architect:** dwp

"Rest Detail: A hotel where every detail, no matter how small, really matters"

Rest Detail Hotel was built in Modern Oriental style inspired by Hua Hin's very own ambience and employing the finest local materials with an eye to detail. It is spacious, open and airy, and decorated with colours in keeping with the tropical seaside, together with such chic touches as tile mosaics, stunning chandeliers, waterfall features and outdoor Jacuzzis, double daybeds built out over the swimming pool, and individual letterboxes for each room.

Every detail is anticipated to ensure a true surrender to the charms of this tropical seaside resort, encompassing body, mind and soul. There is also an added detail in mood; as joyful and refreshing as the resort's logo of The Three Wise Monkeys, which symbolize living a wise life and closing ourselves off from the sights and sounds of the busy outside world so as to relax and take time out.

## Address
19/119, Moo Baan Bor Fai (Soi Hua Hin 19), Hua Hin, Prachuap Khiri Khan, 77110
**T:** +66 (0) 3257 4733, **F:** +66 (0) 3257 4722, **E:** rest@restdetailhotel.com
www.restdetailhotel.com

# Piman Plearnwan
## พิมานเพลินวาน

**Type:** Hotel
**Style:** Vintage
**Room type:** 20 Rooms; 18 Classic Rooms, 2 Deluxe Rooms
**Room rate:** 3,200 to 3,700 THB
**Facilities:** Restaurant
**Architect, Interior and Landscape Architect:** Openbox

Imagine travelling to an old town to indulge nostalgic memories amid the atmospheric scenery of a wooden shop-house and folk market. All around are colorful Thai festive decorations and the sounds of the good old days. When night falls, move up from the lively ground floor to the second floor where there are quiet, cozy rooms painted in light colours and furnished in neo-antique style, just like visiting grandma's sitting room. Such sequences of experiences fired the imagination of a combined design team to create Piman Plearnwan.

Via a staircase leading up to the second floor, guests walk through an open-air corridor decorated in an artistic concept of 50s' retro style. Retro style wallpaper, pastel colour timber walls and framed historic pictures, all set the mood and tone of a classic bygone era. Every décor item and piece of furniture was either made or selected to be unique yet functional.

**Address**

4/90-95, Baan Bo Fai, Phetkasem Road, Hua Hin, Prachuap Khiri Khan, 77110

**T:** +66 (0) 3252 0311-2, **F:** +66 (0) 3252 0317, **E:** reservations@plearnwan.com

www.plearnwan.com

# The Herbs by the Sea Hotel and Spa

เดอะ เฮิบส์ บาย เดอะ ซี โฮเท็ล แอนด์ สปา

**Type:** Boutique Hotel and Spa
**Style:** Lanna-Contemporary
**Room type:** 9 Rooms; 3 Superior Rooms, 4 Deluxe Rooms, 2 Suite Rooms
**Room rate:** 4,000 to 8,000 THB
**Facilities:** Pool
**Interior Architect:** Pinit Foungchan

The Herbs by the Sea is an old seaside home, located on a beautiful beach, which has been converted and redecorated as a luxurious boutique hotel. The name 'Herbs' was inspired by the plants' renowned healing abilities, the use of herbs for healing being by far the world's oldest and most widely known therapy. From this, along with the founder's 25-year background in cosmetics and herbal products, the 'Herbs' concept was developed.

Featuring contemporary Lanna-style, all The Herbs' rooms boast the perfect composition of wooden furniture, timber window and door frames, brushed concrete walls and floors, and metal appliances. Moreover, being herbal themed, each room's décor, scent and colour scheme are evocative of a different herb, as in, for example, 'The Bergamot', 'The Chamomile', and 'The Lavender' rooms. Guests can also indulge their senses with exotic Thai herbal and aroma treatments.

**Address**

1/12 Naebkhehars Road, Hua Hin, Prachuap Khiri Khan, 77110

**T:** +66 (0) 3251 2289, **F:** +66 (0) 3251 3935, **E:** theherbshotel@gmail.com

www.theherbshotel.com

# DUNE
#### hua-hin

# Dune Hua Hin Hotel
### โรงแรมดูนน์ หัวหิน

**Type:** Boutique Hotel
**Style:** Modern
**Room type:** 5 Rooms; 2 Superior Rooms, 2 Deluxe Rooms, 1 Dune Suite
**Room Rate:** 5,100 to 15,800 THB
**Facilities:** Pool, Spa, Restaurant, Bar
**Architect:** Be Gray
**Interior Architect:** GIM Design

Dune Hua Hin Hotel is a small exclusive beach boutique hotel offering five modern stylish rooms and the utmost personalized service. You will be indulged with privacy and peace enjoyed in the comfort of fully-equipped accommodation, while a lovely beach is only a stone's throw away.

The interior decoration is minimalist in style, but with a fine touch of detail to meet the demands of a contemporary, luxurious lifestyle. The Dune suite, with a private pool, has a casual yet elegant design in its black and grey interior. Alternatively, a deluxe room with a beige and cream interior creates a warm sense of comfort and radiates a stylish ambience. Indeed, all the interior décor is meticulously finished with fine details, ranging from textured walls to linen backdrops.

Overall, a modern comfort living area oozes simplicity and shows off minimalist decoration with lavish detail. Among notable individual features is a black giant Serralunga, designed by Rodolfo Dordoni, which has been modified with a light touch of Oriental style to be used as a traditional Thai bathtub.

**Address**
Soi Hua Hin 45, Naebkhehars Road, Hua Hin, Prachuap Khiri Khan, 77110
**T:** +66 (0) 3251 5051-3, **F:** +66 (0) 3251 5052, **E:** reservation@dunehuahin.com
www.dunehuahin.com

The hen

# The Hen Hua Hin
### เดอะ เฮน หัวหิน

**Type:** Boutique Resort
**Style:** Modern Vintage
**Room type:** 6 Rooms; 1 Pool View Room, 2 Sea View Rooms, 2 Pool Villas, 1 Honeymoon Suite
**Room rate:** 4,990 to 15,900 THB
**Facilities:** Pool
**Architect, Interior and Landscape Architect:** Suranard Lerdkunakorn

Originally a private bungalow built during the reign of King Rama VII, this one-storey villa was once the summer vacation home of the Diskul royal family and enjoys an exclusive location that still retains a classic air.

The owner of The Hen is also a designer fascinated by antique styles and has renovated this historic building to recreate Hua Hin's traditional ambience of ease. The decor is a combination of vintage white and colonial furnishings, as exemplified in a European style living room with high ceilings, tall windows, painted glazed floor tiles, bathtub with lion shaped pedestals, ceiling fan, and chandeliers.

The open courtyard is paved in a checkered pattern and is distinctive for an antique Chinese bed in the center that becomes a sofa during the day. Set in this area, surrounded by tropical plants, are the main pool and a Jacuzzi, which uses a salt-water chlorinator system that is both refreshing and environmentally friendly.

All rooms are, naturally, named after chickens, such as the Hen, the Rooster, the Pleiades, the Chick, and the Pullet, and many decorative motifs reflect the theme.

**Address**
31 (Samnak Diskul), Naebkhehars Road, Hua Hin, Prachuap Khiri Khan, 77110
**T:** +66 (0) 3253 1331, **F:** +66 (0) 3253 1146, **E:** info@thehenhuahin.com
www.thehenhuahin.com

PUTAHRACSA
HUA HIN

# Putahracsa Hua Hin

### พุทธรักษา หัวหิน

**Type:** Boutique Resort

**Style:** Contemporary

**Room type:** 59 Units; 36 Silk Sand Rooms, 8 Sand Sky Villas, 7 Ocean Bed Jacuzzi Villas,
5 Ocean Bed Pool Villas, 2 La Canna Pool Villas, 1 La Canna Beachfront Villa

**Room Rate:** 4,000 to 27,000 THB

**Facilities:** Pool, Spa, Restaurant, Bar, Library

**Architect:** Design Scene (Main Wing), BAB (Oceanside Wing)

**Interior Architect:** Viboon Techakalayatum

Putahracsa is a luxury low-rise resort offering a refined experience that does away with the usual limitations of other hotels and allows guests to personalize their stay according to their own desires.

The resort has been designed in contemporary style with minimalist themes, and features unique layouts and neutral materials and colours. The 59 units are separated into two wings, the Main Wing being set amidst a lush garden, where rooms and villas stand aside the swimming pool, while the Oceanside Wing offers luxury and privacy with astonishing views of the sea.

Guests can indulge in relaxing massages and other health treatments at Putahracsa's day spa, or enjoy quiet moments in the resort's library. For a more active time, opportunities include hiking or a round of golf at a nearby course.

**Address**

22/65, Neabkhehars Road, Hua Hin, Prachuap Khiri Khan, 77110

**T:** +66 (0) 3253 1470, **F:** +66 (0) 3253 1488, **E:** info@putahracsa.com

www.putahracsa.com

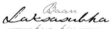

# Baan Laksasubha Resort Hua Hin

บ้าน ลักษสุภา รีสอร์ท หัวหิน

**Type:** Resort

**Style:** Traditional Thai Nobility Villas

**Room type:** Garden View, Garden Veranda, Garden Suite One Bedroom, Garden Suite Two Bedrooms, Garden Villa

**Room rate:** 6,500 to 22,100 THB

**Facilities:** Pool, Spa, Restaurant, Bar

**Interior Architect:** M.L. Laksasubha Kridakon

**Landscape Architect:** Abha Kridakon

An ideal getaway from the heat of Bangkok for more than over 70 years, Baan Laksasubha is part of Hua Hin's heritage as a royal retreat. Created by owner M.L. Laksasubha Kridakon, the great granddaughter of HRH Prince Krisda Bhiniharn, who was the first to build a royal summer home in Hua Hin, this colonial-style resort is a place to relax amid secluded surroundings and an air of nostalgia.

Baan Laksasubha consists of 16 two-story villas, each with a spacious upper terrace and set in its own lush landscaped garden within the same grounds as the owner's original family home, which creates a cozy environment. The mix-and-match interior decoration combines old and new furniture in a colour scheme of predominantly white and blue, while the décor reflects a traditional lifestyle influenced by the Thai nobility. First-class services and facilities are specifically designed to meet all guests' needs.

**Address**
53/7, Naresdamri Road, Hua Hin, Prachuap Khiri Khan, 77110
**T:** +66 (0) 3251 4525-31, **F:** +66 (0) 3251 4532, **E:** rsvn@baanlaksasubha.com
www.baanlaksasubha.com

£529.00 a wk.

# Baan Bayan Beach Hotel
## บ้านบาหยัน

**Type:** Boutique Hotel
**Style:** Colonial-style beach house
**Room type:** 1 House and 21 Rooms; 5 Garden View Rooms, 9 Courtyard View Rooms,
2 Sea View Rooms, 2 Sea View Villas, 1 Irada Suite Room, 1 Bannika Suite Room, 1 Taraban Suite Room
**Room rate:** 4,800++ to 28,400++ THB
**Facilities:** Pool, Spa, Restaurant, Bar
**Architect:** Dr. Yuwarat Hemasilpin
**Interior and Landscape Architect:** W.H. Associates

Baan Bayan was originally built in the early 1900's as a royal family's summer retreat. Later, in order to preserve this historic house for future generations, the owners decided to turn their property into a small hotel and so ensure its ongoing maintenance.

The house, as well as its surroundings, which include a hundred-year-old frangipani tree and a ground-water well, was thus restored to its original state. Only a few amenities were added to give modern comforts, such as bathrooms and air-conditioning. To serve more guests, five new buildings were constructed with a courtyard creating an airy space between them.

The spatial organization of the interiors, however, hasn't been changed. The breezy verandah facing the beach is still a gathering space, and the multi-purpose space beneath a raised floor has been used as a dining area since early days.

The colour combination of the new buildings was chosen both to reflect the pastel shades of the historic house and to brighten the scene. Much simpler wooden railings were used in the new buildings in contrast to the flamboyant details of the original ones. The furnishing comprises refurbished original items, ranging from colonial style to the art deco, while guestrooms have been decorated by combining southern-Thai batik fabrics with abstract oil paintings in harmonious colours but contrasting styles.

In 2005, Baan Bayan was awarded the prestigious Historical Architectural Conservation Award by the Association of Siamese Architects (ASA) under the Royal Patronage.

**Address**
119, Phetkasem Road, Hua Hin, Prachuap Khiri Khan, 77110
**T:** +66 (0) 3253 3544, **F:** +66 (0) 3253 3545, **E:** sales@baanbayan.com
www.beachfronthotelhuahin.com

# AKA Resort Guti Hua Hin & AKA Resort Hua Hin

อาคารีสอร์ท กุฏิ หัวหิน และ อาคารีสอร์ท หัวหิน

**Type:** Resort

**Style:** Contemporary Thai & Traditional Chinese

**Room type:** (AKA Resort Guti Hua Hin) 19 Units; One-bedroom Pool Villa 7 Units, Two-bedroom Deluxe Pool Villa 12 Units

(AKA Resort Hua Hin) 48 Units; One-bedroom Pool Villa 3 Units, One-bedroom Deluxe Pool Villa 35 Units, Two-bedroom Deluxe Pool Villa 10 Units

**Room rate:** (AKA Resort Guti Hua Hin) start from 26,305 THB

(AKA Resort Hua Hin) start from 24,305 THB

**Facilities:** Pool, Spa, Restaurant, Lounge, Bar, Fitness, Library

**Architect and Interior Architect:** Trend Design

Based on a love of nature, the AKA philosophy is one of providing an oasis in which to relax and revitalize Thus AKA Resort Guti, nestling against a gentle hillside, is a hideaway with privacy and closeness to nature that presents its guests with a healing, harmonious and intimate lifestyle in discreet villas.

Designed by an architect of internationally acclaimed spa resorts, AKA Resort Guti is in contemporary Thai style with traditional Chinese influences, and blends ancient and modern to give interiors that mix and match contemporary and local materials such as teak, bamboo and Thai silk.

With an emphasis on the utmost privacy and attention to detail, guest villas are dotted around 25 acres of a verdant tropical landscape, sheltered by mountains and commanding panoramic views of the countryside. Facilities include a private 10-metre infinity-edge pool, garden terrace, private courtyard, and elegant Thai pavilion.

Just 1.5 km away from AKA Resort Guti is AKA Resort Hua Hin, which has been voted among the Top Ten Boutique Resorts in South East Asia. Nestling reclusively against a gentle hillside, its architecture and interior design are simple and sustainable, created with local materials and craftsmanship. Set in a 10-acre site, the resort's private villas showcase elegant design and modern amenities, providing guests with a private oasis amidst Thailand's tropical landscape.

Reflecting Hua Hin's cultural heritage, AKA Resort Hua Hin is a rejuvenating and luxurious retreat from the stresses of daily life. Each deluxe villa is infused with an ambience of tranquility and combines luxurious interiors with a 10-metre private infinity-edge swimming pool, garden sunken bath & shower, sundeck, and terraced courtyard with a Thai pavilion.

Both AKA Resort Hua Hin and AKA Resort Guti are members of Small Luxury Hotels of the World (SLH)

**Address**
152, Moo 7, Baan Nhong Hiang, Hin Lek Fai, Hua Hin, Prachuap Khiri Khan, 77110
**T:** +66 (0) 3261 8900, **F:** +66 (0) 3261 8999, **E:** info@akaresorts.com
www.akaresorts.com

The lifestyle and local culture of Hua Hin, Cha-am, and Pranburi are a reflection of their being originally fishing communities, and the tradition survives. Although some fishermen's houses have been transformed into restaurants or shop-houses for economic reasons, there are still many working fishing villages and fish piers that are tourist attractions. Should one like to experience the local way of life, the 65-year-old Chatchai Market is a place where people take a stroll and look through various local products ranging from dried seafood to Khomapastr printed fabric, while multiple choices of street food await to be tasted in the evening.

Another place worth visiting is Hua Hin railway station, located not far from Chatchai Market. The place preserves its old style of architecture and also has on display a WWII steam locomotive. To travel to these places is easily done by hiring a trishaw to drive around and absorb the town atmosphere.

# Southern Hua Hin

**Gulf of Thailand**

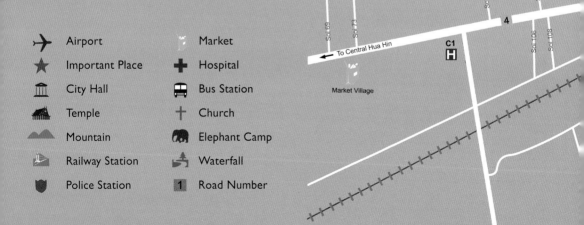

| | | | |
|---|---|---|---|
| ✈ Airport | | 🛍 Market | |
| ★ Important Place | | ✚ Hospital | |
| 🏛 City Hall | | 🚌 Bus Station | |
| 🏯 Temple | | ✝ Church | |
| ⛰ Mountain | | 🐘 Elephant Camp | |
| 🚉 Railway Station | | 💧 Waterfall | |
| 🛡 Police Station | | **1** Road Number | |

To Central Hua Hin

Market Village

C1 **H**

C2 **H**

4

Soi 59

Soi 73

Soi 83

Soi 85

Soi 106

Soi 108

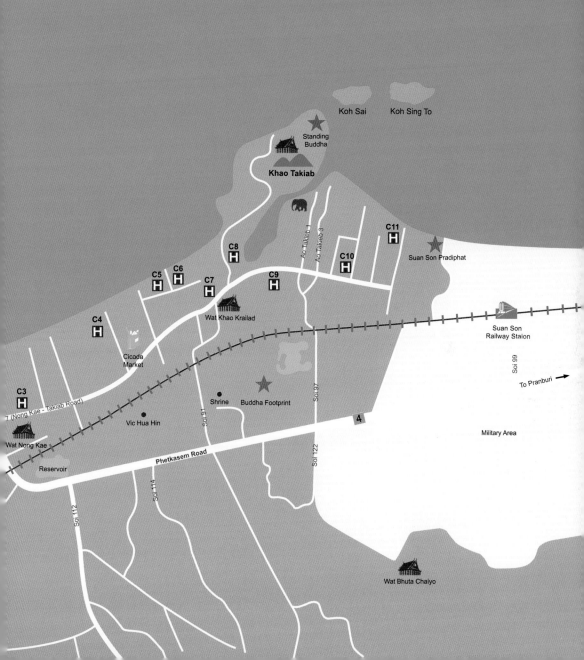

Koh Sai

Koh Sing To

Standing Buddha

**Khao Takiab**

C11

C8

Suan Son Pradiphat

C5

C6

C10

C4

C7

C9

Wat Khao Krailad

Ao Takiab 1

Ao Takiab 3

Soi 97

Suan Son Railway Staion

Soi 99

To Pranburi

Cicada Market

C3

Shrine

Buddha Footprint

7 (Nong Kae - Takiab Road)

Vic Hua Hin

Soi 91

4

Military Area

Wat Nong Kae

Phetkasem Road

Reservoir

Soi 112

Soi 114

Soi 122

Wat Bhuta Chaiyo

**The Lapa**
HUA HIN

# The Lapa Hua Hin
เดอะ ลาภา หัวหิน

**Type:** Boutique Hotel
**Style:** Contemporary
**Room type:** 31 Rooms; 17 Lapa Superior Rooms, 4 Lapa Delite Rooms, 4 Lapa Cool Rooms,
3 Lapa Terrace Suite Rooms, 3 Lapa Duplex Suite Rooms
**Room rate:** 7,200++ to 21,000++ THB
**Facilities:** Pool, Pool Bar, Spa, Restaurant, Fitness, Library
**Architect and Landscape Architect:** Agora
**Interior Architect:** Gub and Cushion & Curtain by Passaya

The Lapa is a new breed of hotel; a design-led environment created for discerning travellers. Located in the heart of the royal resort town of Hua Hin, The Lapa provides guests with a chic and exclusive retreat.

Attention to detail is what gives the Lapa its strength. Clean lines, exquisite minimalist interiors, and refreshing open spaces combine to form a cool and relaxed environment. A blend of dark woods, white-washed walls, and earthy tones is complemented by splashes of turquoise and blue. It all adds up to a subtle marine feel, evoking a luxurious beachside ambience. Bathed in natural light, rooms feature tropical-inspired décor, outstanding furnishings, and eye-catching design accents.

At the center is a large swimming pool, the first in Hua Hin to be treated with ozone and salt and complete with a jet stream, is set amid lush gardens and blossoming flowers. Just a few metres away from the pool, are two superior rooms with a private mock sandy beach.

**Address**
4/115, Soi Mooban Nong Kae, Nong Kae, Hua Hin, Prachuap Khiri Khan, 77110
**T:** +66 (0) 3251 3222, **F:** +66 (0) 3251 6715, **E:** rm@thelapahotel.com
www.thelapahotel.com

**VILLAS**
HUA HIN

# V Villas Hua Hin
## Managed by Accor

โรงแรม วี วิลล่า หัวหิน

**Type:** Hotel & Resort
**Style:** Contemporary
**Room type:** 13 Villas; Two-bedroom Pool Villa Suite 10 Units,
Three-bedroom Pool Villa Suite 2 Units, The Presidential Beachfront Pool Villa Suite 1 Unit
**Room rate:** start from 36,017 THB
**Facilities:** Pool, Spa, Restaurant, Bar, Fitness, Library
**Architect and Interior Architect:** Design Collaboration
between J+H Boiffils and The Office of Bangkok Architects (OBA)
**Landscape Architect:** Belt Collins International (Thailand)

V Villas comes from the creative vision of renowned French architectural design company J+H Boiffils. Drawing inspiration from the geometric patterns of terraced rice paddies and the sophistication of European Villazzos, the result is a refined contemporary lifestyle resort for well-travelled and sophisticated individuals.

At V Villas, bold lines and architectural symmetry contrast with natural elements to create a visually intriguing and relaxed environment. This premium-class resort sits beautifully on a site that connects directly to Hua Hin beach. Intended for upper-income guests, the resort is designed for exclusivity. Each unit has its own living space, private swimming pool and garden, and spacious en suite bathroom. The planning solution perfectly solves the privacy issue and isolates the service areas from the public spaces. Guests can enjoy the luxury of outstanding facilities, amenities, and service that includes butlers on hand day and night.

### Address

Moobaan Nong Kae, Nong Kae, Hua Hin, Prachuap Khiri Khan, 77110

**T:** +66 (0) 3261 6039, **F:** +66 (0) 3251 2042, **E:** info@vvillashuahin.com

www.v-villashuahin.com

# Chiva-Som

ชีวาศรม

**Type:** Destination Spa
**Style:** Modern-Traditional Thai
**Room type:** 58 Rooms; 33 Ocean View Rooms, 17 Thai Pavilion Rooms, 2 Herbal Suite Rooms,
2 Fragance Suite Rooms, 2 Rain Forest Suite Rooms, 1 Golden Bo Suite Room, 1 Leelawadee Suite Room
**Room rate:** start from 61,380 to 68,310 THB for 3 nights in Ocean View Room
**Facilities:** Pool, Spa, Restaurant, Fitness
**Architect and Interior Architect:** Syntax and Trend Design
**Landscape Architect:** In & Out Landscape

A secluded world of beauty and serenity, Chiva-Som is the 'Haven of Life'. Located in the royal city of Hua Hin and set within seven acres of lush tropical gardens, this beachfront resort represents tranquility at its best, with luxurious accommodation inspired by a harmonious blend of East and West.

Established some 15 years ago, Chiva-Som was Thailand's first luxury destination spa and it maintains a unique dedication to total wellness through its comprehensive and extensive services ranging from nurturing spa to high-tech medical. The quality of the facilities is matched by the world-class caliber of its practitioners and therapists, as well as by its inimitable Thai hospitality. Grounded firmly in the belief that it is the combined health of the mind, body and spirit that leads to personal fulfillment, Chiva-Som is truly holistic in its approach and is one of the most awarded health resorts in the world.

Incorporated with the concept of 'traditional Asian therapies with Western health and wellness', Chiva-Som is designed and decorated using a combination of Thai and western architecture, adapting of old forms to new needs in a very personalized way and using the finest local materials and craftsmanship.

**Address**
73/4, Phetkasem Road, Hua Hin, Prachuap Khiri Khan, 77110
**T:** +66 (0) 3253 6536, **F:** +66 (0) 3251 1154, **E:** reservation@chivasom.com
www.chivasom.com

# The Barai

## เถอะ บาราย

**Type:** Resort & Spa
**Style:** Dramatic Architecture with Touches of Heritage of South East Asia
**Room type:** 8 Residential Spa Suites, 18 Exotic Treatment Rooms
**Room rate:** start from 15,800 THB
**Facilities:** Pool, Spa, Restaurant, Fitness
**Architect and Interior Architect:** Bunnag Architects
**Landscape Architect:** Bensley Design Studio

The Barai, a residential spa, is located on more than 4.5 acres of serene beachfront land adjacent to Hyatt Regency Hua Hin and is landscaped with lush gardens, manicured lawns, picturesque fountains and a lagoon. It promises a journey of the mind, body and spirit guided by stylish Oriental architecture. The goal of the journey is a delightful feeling of peace and tranquility deep within your inner self. Art is the defining aspect of the architecture, which aims to create moods and have an emotional impact.

The key design element in the project is light, strong and romantic, accompanied by shadow to create surprises, a sense of wonder, and a sense of place.

The hotel enjoys a 250-metre beachfront, the longest of any resort in Hua Hin, and offers a holistic approach to wellness and inner tranquility. An extensive range of custom-designed spa treatments, echoing every personal need and desire, allows everyone to create the journey that is best suited to their body, mind and spirit. This is truly a special spa and hotel, a tranquil and spiritual sanctuary with luxurious accommodation.

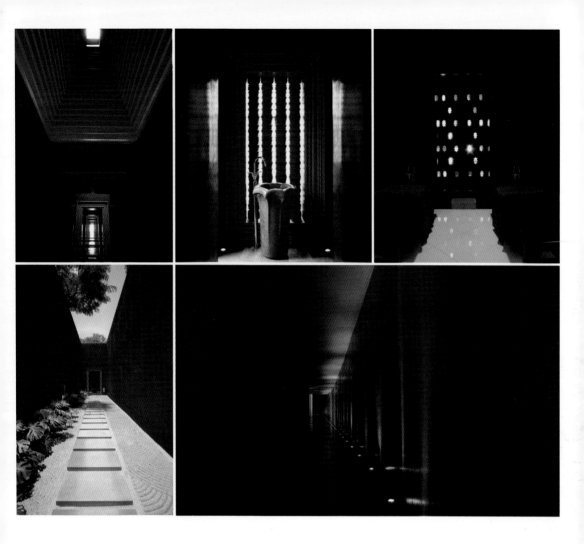

**Address**
91, Hua Hin – Khao Takiab Road, Hua Hin, Prachuap Khiri Khan, 77110
**T:** +66 (0) 3252 1234, **F:** +66 (0) 3252 1233, **E:** thebarai.hrhuahin@hyatt.com
www.thebarai.com

# Hua Hin Mantra Resort

### หัวหิน มันตรา รีสอร์ท

**Type:** Boutique Resort
**Style:** Contemporary Thai
**Room type:** Deluxe Room, Deluxe Panorama Sea View Room,
Super Deluxe Room, Premium Suite Room
**Room rate:** 2,690++ to 3,390++ THB
**Facilities:** Pool, Restaurant, Bar,

Hua Hin Mantra is a contemporary Thai-style boutique hotel offering a simple and peaceful escape amid tropical surroundings that fully reflect Hua Hin's traditional charm. Located near Khao Takiab, the resort has private access to a beautiful unspoiled white sandy beach just a minute's walk away.

All rooms are spacious and tastefully decorated with Khomapastr, a local fabric that has long been the pride of Hua Hin, while facilities include a large outdoor swimming pool, whirlpool Jacuzzi, pool b ar, sun deck, and traditional Thai massage. Surrounded by tropical plants and herbs, Hua Hin Mantra Resort captivates with its ambience of a tropical paradise in which to relish peace and tranquillity.

**Address**
83/181, Phetkasem Road, Nong Kae, Hua Hin, Prachuap Khiri Khan, 77110
**T:** +66 (0) 3253 6777, **F:** +66 (0) 3253 6777, **E:** info@huahinmantra.com
www.huahinmantra.com

# Let's Sea Hua Hin
## Al Fresco Resort
### เล็ตส์ ซี หัวหิน

**Type:** Resort
**Style:** Seaside Al Fresco
**Room type:** 40 Rooms; 20 Studio Pier Rooms, 20 Moon Deck Suite Rooms
**Room rate:** start from 11,111 THB
**Facilities:** Pool, Spa, Restaurant, Lounge, Bar, Fitness
**Architect:** Gaia & Agaligo
**Interior Architect:** Suchanoot Saengrungrueng
**Landscape Architect:** Busakorn Bunnag

Let's Sea Hua Hin Al Fresco Resort combines romance, intuitive service and thoughtfully designed facilities to create a memorable yet accessible escape. It also captures the quiet charm of Hua Hin which, as a long-time favorite seaside destination, still retains a quiet, unassuming appeal. The resort's architect referenced this and other characteristics of the Thai holiday lifestyle to create a unique resort environment along one of the area's most desirable and peaceful stretches of beach.

Its 40 spacious retreats include some unforgettable touches. In 'Studio Piers' on the first floor, for example, guests can enjoy their own personal pier access to the canal-like swimming pool, while in the 'Moon Deck Suite' guests have their own romantic open-air deck, as well as easy access to the pool.

All the intuitively designed rooms feature the ultimate in beach vacation comfort, from the Let's Sea 'laZzzzz' bed and mood lighting to the extensive terrazzo bathroom with an oversized tub and separate rain shower for two, while in-room technology is at your fingertips. Also, Let's Sea Al Fresco's lifestyle is energy efficient due to clever energy saving architecture that takes advantage of natural light and beach breezes.

**Address**
83/155, Soi Talay 12, Khao Takiab – Hua Hin Road, Nong Kae, Hua Hin, Prachuap Khiri Khan, 77110
**T:** +66 (0) 3253 6888, **F:** +66 (0) 3253 6887, **E:** info.huahin@letussea.com
www.letussea.com

# The Rock Hua Hin Beach Resort
เดอะร็อค หัวหิน บีช รีสอร์ต

**Type:** Boutique Resort

**Style:** Contemporary

**Room type:** 25 Rooms; 4 Deluxe Rooms, 12 Exclusive Deluxe Rooms,
7 Deluxe Suites Rooms, 1 Bedroom Sea View Villa, 1 Twin Bedroom Villa

**Room rate:** 4,500 to 19,200 THB

**Facilities:** Pool, Restaurant, Bar

The Rock Hua Hin Beach Resort, set on one of Hua Hin's finest beaches close to Khao Takiab, is a small luxury resort that blends ethnic and contemporary style. All rooms are delicately designed under the concept of blending Thai and Mediterranean luxury to give an ideal sense of a relaxing retreat.

The 26 executive rooms are located in a detached low-rise building set in tropical gardens. Each room is richly appointed with custom-made furniture and luxurious décor, and all rooms have either a king-size or two double beds with comfortable duvets. Most rooms also have an open-style bathroom. Spacious private balconies and/or sun lounges, along with an infinity-edge pool, enhance the sense of a romantic retreat.

**Address**
4/44, Moo Baan Takiab Road, Hua Hin, Prachuap Khiri Khan, 77110
**T:** +66 (0) 3253 7100, **F:** +66 (0) 3253 7108, **E:** info@therockhuahin.com
www.therockhuahin.com

830.73 christmas wk

# Supatra Hua Hin Resort

สุภัทรา หัวหิน รีสอร์ต

**Type:** Boutique Hotel
**Style:** Tropical
**Room type:** 18 Rooms; 1 Superior Pool Villa, 1 Pool Villa,
3 Sea View Units, 13 Garden View Rooms
**Room rate:** 3,000 to 11,000 THB
**Facilities:** Pool, Restaurant, Bar
**Architect:** M.L. Sudavdee Kriangkrai

A place of great charm, Supatra Hua Hin Resort is located at the base of Khao Takiab, where a giant golden Buddha faces east across the sea. The lush and beautiful gardens that surround the property, accompanied by the sounds of the ocean, provide a comfortable, quiet and relaxing atmosphere.

The resort offers many different styles of living in traditional Thai elegance, along with all modern amenities such as Wi-Fi, and includes a unique bungalow with separate private access to the beach. Each room combines wood with smooth terracotta tiled floors, sliding glass doors, gentle stone showers, and bold wooden beams.

With sprawling gardens and a beachfront pool, guests can enjoy a beautiful tropical setting that exudes a tranquil ambience. Complementing the comfort of luxurious accommodation is the Thai tradition of friendly, yet unobtrusive service.

**Address**

143/18, Takiab Road, Nong Kae, Hua Hin, Prachuap Khiri Khan, 77110
**T:** +66 (0) 3253 6893-4, **F:** +66 (0) 3253 6895, **E:** supatraresort@hotmail.com
www.supatraresort.com

# Seahorse Resort
## ซีฮอส รีสอร์ท

**Type:** Boutique Resort
**Style:** Ethnoriental
**Room type:** 31 Rooms; 10 Malibu Rooms, 10 Terrace Rooms, 8 White Vista Rooms,
2 Exotic Rooms, 1 Party Room
**Room rate:** 2,500 to 6,500 THB
**Facilities:** Pool, Bar
**Architect and Interior Architect:** mooof
**Landscape Architect:** Chawalit Tongloun

The style of Seahorse Resort is 'ethnoriental', a mix of Mediterranean and Oriental influences. White and blue are contrasted with pink to give an atmospheric effect, as in the colour of coral, while spaces are created with simplicity of form and natural textures.

Interior styles differ by room category. Malibu, for example, is decorated with a colour plane frame and rustic texture, while an outer gradation of blue creates a sea effect. The bathroom comes with natural light through a lattice shade.

Moon Terrace rooms, with a big bed terrace on the upper floor, are in different colour tones from a range of five – green, orange, yellow, purple and blue. White Vista, the grand suite with private Jacuzzi, is decorated entirely in white but with colored lighting selected to create mood. Exotic, family-style accommodation, offers two bedrooms and a double space living area that connects with an upper, attic-like bedroom.

**Address**
123/45, Moo Baan Takiab, Nong Kae, Hua Hin, Prachuap Khiri Khan, 77110
**T:** +66 (0) 3253 7111, **F:** +66 (0) 3253 7111, **E:** info@seahorse-resort.com
www.seahorse-resort.com

# Riad Hua Hin

ริยาจ หัวหิน

**Type:** Boutique Resort

**Style:** Moroccan

**Room type:** 12 Rooms; 2 Sleeping Cat Rooms, 4 Sitting Cat with Balcony Rooms, 2 Sitting Cat without Balcony Rooms, 4 Standing Cat Rooms

**Room rate:** 2,400 to 3,200 THB

**Facilities:** Pool

**Architect, Interior and Landscape Architect:** Life Image

Riad's design concept was inspired by the distinctive architecture of Morocco, the resort's name in Arabic meaning a traditional Moroccan house or palace with an interior garden or courtyard.

The orange-yellow architecture envelops the interior facilities, which are focused on a central pool with lobby and lounge surrounding. The guest room in the L-shaped building has been designed to give full play to the natural breezes and morning sunlight, while the antique furniture and colourful décor elements create a rich sense of the exotic.

To emphasize the warmth and charm of its atmosphere, Riad takes the cat as a symbol and staying here you can feel the feline's dignity on the outside, but its very playfulness inside.

**Address**
75, Hua Don Village, Hua Hin, Prachuap Khiri Khan, 77110
**T:** +66 (0) 3253 6954, **F:** +66 (0) 3253 6827, **E:** reservation@riadhuahin.com
www.riadhuahin.com

# The Bihai Hua Hin
### เดอะ ไบฮาย หัวหิน

**Type:** Boutique Hotel
**Style:** Modern Contemporary
**Room type:** 15 Rooms; 5 Pool Terrace Rooms, 2 @ Sea Rooms, 4 Sea View Rooms, 4 Deluxe Rooms
**Room rate:** 2,990 to 4,100 THB
**Facilities:** Pool, Roof Top Pool, Restaurant
**Architect:** Varakorn Techamontrikul, Jirut Sampanyooth
**Interior Architect:** Khwantip Kaongern
**Landscape Architect:** Jirut Sampanyooth

The Bihai is an exclusive beachside hotel occupying an attractive modern building, nestling comfortably in its natural surroundings. From the beginning, the Bihai was created to accommodate guests who look for quiet and privacy. It is like living in a home villa, although full hotel services are offered.

Wood and other natural materials have been chosen for the decoration and furnishing of the rooms, with, for example, white polished stone floors, chic dark wood furniture and crisp white cotton sheets, to offer an atmosphere of quiet sophistication. There is an emphasis on clean lines and a warm, inviting minimalism, while huge windows and generously sized balconies expand the sea and mountain views. It all makes for a wonderful romantic escape, a chance for privacy and tranquility away from the crowds. Not least, this intimate scale ensures highly personalized service.

### Address

89, Moo 5, Baan Hua Don, Takiab Road, Nong Kae, Hua Hin, Prachuap Khiri Khan, 77110

**T:** +66 (0) 3252 7557-9, **F:** +66 (0) 3252 7556, **E:** info@thebihaihuahin.com

www.thebihaihuahin.com

National Parks are a further attraction, two notably examples being found not far from the white sand beaches of Hua Hin, Cha-am, and Pranburi. These are Kaeng Krachan National Park, one of Thailand's largest, and Khao Sam Roi Yot National Park, which was the country's first marine national park. These preserves maintain the balance of nature by nurturing river, forest and mountain habitats that are home to various species of animals and plants. There are also waterfalls and several beautiful caves.

Off the coast, islands are scattered across the Gulf and include Koh Singh, Koh Sung, Koh Talu, and Koh Lumra, which lie within the coral reef intertidal area. Tourists can thus vary their enjoyment and switch their time from lazing by the sea to hiking through nature.

# Pranburi
## Sam Roi Yot - Kui Buri - Thap Sakae

- H **D1** Pran-A-Luxe
- H **D2** Villa Maroc Resort, Pranburi
- H **D3** Foresta Resort Pranburi
- H **D4** Ali Baba Resort Pranburi
- H **D5** Aleenta Resort & Spa, Hua Hin - Pranburi
- H **D6** Praseban Resort
- H **D7** The Bayburi Vacation Villas Hua Hin
- H **D8** Purimantra Resort and Spa
- H **D9** La a Natu Bed & Bakery
- H **D10** Brassiere Beach Resort
- H **D11** X2 Hua Hin Kui Buri
- H **D12** Nisha Ville Resort and Spa

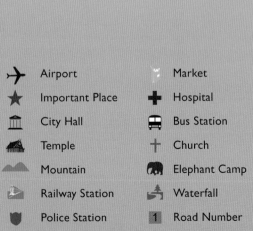

| Symbol | Legend | Symbol | Legend |
|---|---|---|---|
| ✈ | Airport | | Market |
| ★ | Important Place | ✚ | Hospital |
| 🏛 | City Hall | 🚌 | Bus Station |
| 🛕 | Temple | ✝ | Church |
| ⛰ | Mountain | 🐘 | Elephant Camp |
| | Railway Station | | Waterfall |
| | Police Station | 1 | Road Number |

Khao Tao
Soi 101
Shrine
By Pass To Hua Hin
Paknam Pran
D1
D2
D3
D5
D4
Wat Paknam
Pranburi River
Pranbu
4
Pranburi Railway Station
Phetkasem Road

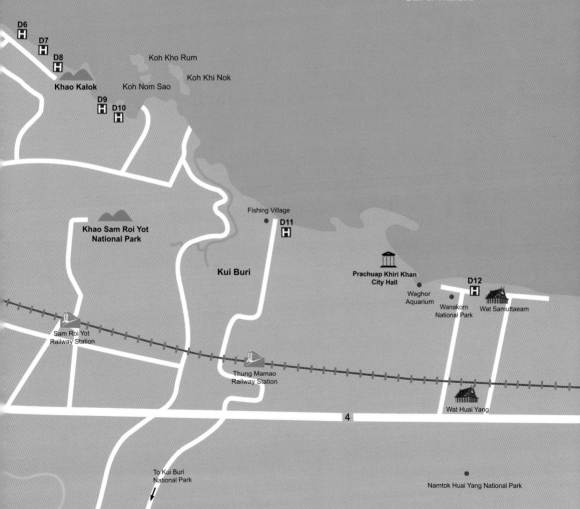

Gulf of Thailand

D6 H

D7 H

D8 H

Khao Kalok

Koh Kho Rum

Koh Khi Nok

Koh Nom Sao

D9 H  D10 H

Khao Sam Roi Yot
National Park

Fishing Village

D11 H

Kui Buri

Prachuap Khiri Khan
City Hall

Waghor
Aquarium

D12 H

Wanakorn
National Park

Wat Samuttaeam

Sam Roi Yot
Railway Station

Thung Mamao
Railway Station

Wat Huai Yang

4

To Kui Buri
National Park

Namtok Huai Yang National Park

# Pran-A-Luxe
ปราณลักษณ์

**Type:** Resort & Residence
**Style:** Tropical Modern
**Room type:** 5 Units; Two-bedroom 1 Unit, Three-bedroom 3 Units, Four-bedroom 1 Unit
**Room rate:** 14,000 to 27,000 THB
**Facilities:** Pool, Fitness
**Architect and Interior Architect:** T-M- Design
**Landscape Architect:** JP Landscape Architect

Pran-A-Luxe offers a selection of different styles of contemporary pool villas, ranging from two to four bedrooms.

An unusual living space is wrapped into a Modern Tropical architectural style, while the creative sea-wave design for the roof presents a unique silhouette. Light is allowed to stream into the interior space via oversized teak doors and windows.

Each villa enjoys its own private swimming pool with multi decking surrounded by a tropical garden. Guests can relax on the sun decks, or take a refreshing dip in the 27-metre infinity edge pool at the Fitness Center.

With its exclusive design, Pran-A-Luxe received the 'Thailand Property Awards 2008 Winner in Best Villa Category'. Beautifully landscaped and harmonizing with nature, these exceptional villas will appeal most especially to the 'Getaway' niche market.

**Address**
454/59-60, Moo 2, Paknam Pran, Pranburi, Prachuap Khiri Khan, 77220
**T:** +66 (0) 3263 1381, **F:** +66 (0) 3263 1382, **E:** info@pranaluxe.com
www.pranaluxe.com

VILLA MAROC
• pranburi •

# Villa Maroc Resort
วิลล่า มาร็อก รีสอร์ท ปราณบุรี

**Type:** Resort & Spa
**Style:** Moroccan
**Room type:** 6 Rooms and 9 Villas; 6 Pool Court Rooms, Pool Villa 4 Units,
One-bedroom Villa 1 Unit, Two-bedroom Villa 2 Units, Royal Villa 2 Units
**Room rate:** 7,900 to 40,500 THB
**Facilities:** Spa, Bar, Fitness
**Architect:** The Office of Bangkok Architect (OBA)
**Interior Architect:** Studio 54
**Landscape Architect:** TLTD Limited (Designfringe)

Villa Maroc is designed to ensure that all accommodation is of the highest standard. With a prime location on a 153-metre stretch of Pranburi coastline, it offers rooms with stunning sea views and direct access to the enticing beach.

Inspired by Morocco's distinctive architecture, Villa Maroc combines Thai beachside living and service with some of the most luxurious furnishings from the North African Kingdom, making it a unique addition to Southeast Asia's accommodation scene.

The resort consists of rooms and villas, all crafted in dramatic Moroccan style with dazzling colours and attention to detail. Each room is creatively named after spices that are such an integral part of Moroccan cuisine and culture. The resort also boasts its own fine dining establishment, Casablanca, located in the courtyard of a traditional Moroccan riad. Just upstairs from the restaurant is Villa Maroc's very own Shisha Bar, the ultimate seaside chill-out lounge serving the coolest cocktails and savory Lebanese mezzehs. For guests looking to indulge and pamper themselves, 'Sherazade Hammam & Spa' is the first authentic hammam in Thailand. Here, amid a combination of the deliciously exotic and the absolutely luxurious, you can experience the very best in Arabic health and beauty treatments.

**Address**
165/3, Moo 3, Paknam Pran, Pranburi, Prachuap Khiri Khan, 77220
**T:** +66 (0) 3263 0771, **F:** +66 (0) 3263 0791, **E:** rsvn@villamarocresort.com
www.villamarocresort.com

# Foresta Resort Pranburi
## ฟอเรสต้า รีสอร์ท ปราณบุรี

**Type:** Boutique Resort
**Style:** Modern Contemporary
**Room type:** 9 Rooms; 2 Superior Rooms, 2 Studio Rooms, 1 Deluxe Room,
2 Pool Side Room, 1 Family Room, 1 Honeymoon Sweet Room
**Room rate:** 1,900 to 6,500 THB
**Facilities:** Pool, Restaurant, Bar
**Architect:** Kowit Kwansrisut

Inspired by images of European houses in a pine forest, Foresta has developed that original idea into the concept 'a hip and cozy resort tucked away amid greenery, although the 'forest' is Indian Cork as pine trees do not grow well in sandy soil.

The first impression created by the resort's ambience is a sense of the forest and the feeling of comfort beneath the shade of large trees. With a modern architectural design, the two-storey buildings are set out with the swimming pool in between. All rooms are decorated in contemporary style with bright colors and cool tones – yellow, green and cyan. Large glass doors welcome in the breeze and views of Pranburi's forest beach, and overall there is a feeling of peace, privacy and the homelike, complemented by Thai hospitality.

**Address**

3, Paknam Pranburi Beach Road, Pranburi, Prachuap Khiri Khan, 77220

**T:** +66 (0) 3263 0678, **F:** +66 (0) 3263 0678, **E:** info@forestaresort.com

www.forestaresort.com

# Ali Baba Resort Pranburi

อาลีบาบา รีสอร์ท ปราณบุรี

**Type:** Boutique Hotel
**Style:** Dubai
**Room type:** 20 Rooms; 10 Fleshly Twin Rooms, 10 Fleshly Twin Rooms
**Room rate:** 1,500 to 2,500 THB
**Facilities:** Pool, Spa, Restaurant, Bar, Fitness, Library
**Architect:** Jarutat Niammanpisut

Ali Baba Resort has a charming location just five minutes walk from Pranburi beach, one of the finest in the whole of Prachuap Khiri Khan province. Local attractions include Pranburi Dam and Khao Sam Roi Yot National Park, while among recreation options are cycling tours and kite boarding.

Opened in May 2009, this boutique resort offers Dubai-style architecture perfectly complemented by a modern interpretation of colonial-period interior décor. The combination, along with bright colours and exotic furnishings, is both welcoming and relaxing.

The accommodation consists of 20 spacious air-conditioned rooms each with twin/double bed, work desk, mini bar, satellite TV, CD/DVD player, Wi-Fi internet, fridge, and tea & coffee making facilities. Non-smoking rooms are available.

## Address
3, Paknam Pranburi Beach Road, Pranburi, Prachuap Khiri Khan, 77220
**T:** +66 (0) 3263 0570, **F:** +66 (0) 3263 0570, **E:** info@alibabaresort.com
www.alibabaresort.com

£128 A WEEK

# △ Aleenta

# Aleenta Resort & Spa,
## Hua Hin - Pranburi

### อลีนตารีสอร์ท แอนด์ สปา, หัวหิน – ปราณบุรี

**Type:** Boutique Resort
**Style:** Mediterranean Coastline
**Room type:** 23 Rooms; 6 Ocean View Suites Rooms,
2 Beach House Suites Rooms, 3 Pool Suites Rooms, 5 Palm Pool Suites Rooms,
1 Penthouse, 2 Frangivaree Suite Rooms, 3 Frangileela Suite Rooms, 1 Chaba Villa
**Room rate:** Start from 4,400 THB
**Facilities:** Pool, Spa, Restaurant, Bar, Library
**Architect, Interior and Landscape Architect:** Simple Space Design

Aleenta Resort and Spa was born out of its owner's love of travel and a quest for a different kind of hotel, where attention to detail rules, where special touches govern, where guests feel special, where small is beautiful. It had to be a place for 'travellers', not 'tourists', in a way a non-hotel. The resulting property first opened its doors in December 2002 with only 10 rooms. Today it has grown to 23 rooms with the addition of converted neighbouring villas.

It is hard to categorize the design of Aleenta as it has grown organically, although the old and new buildings fit well together. The original structure could be termed Mexican, with its salmon pink-burnt sienna colour, while its angles remind you of the Mediterranean coastline. The added new rooms were designed to harmonize, but have a fresher white-on-white tone, while each unique hut has a soft flowing thatched roof adorned with a cone-shaped cap.

Decoration is minimalist as each room's breathtaking sea views make adornment seem superfluous, and the resort's philosophy is 'outside living in', meaning inviting the beauty of outdoors into interior comfort, with no walls where none are needed. Aleenta also encourages its guests reconnect with their inner selves through tranquility – hence a 'no TV' policy.

Aleenta was named by the Far Eastern Economic Review in 2004 as Thailand's first boutique resort, and has subsequently won a number of awards including Conde Nast Traveler Hot List, Wallpaper* Best Room, and Far Eastern Economic Review Top 5 Boutique Resorts in Asia. It is also a member of Small Luxury Hotels of the World (SLH).

**Address**
183, Moo 4, Paknam Pran, Pranburi, Prachuap Khiri Khan, 77220
**T:** +66 (0) 2514 8112, **F:** +66 (0) 2539 4373, **E:** rsvn.hhq@aleenta.com
www.aleenta.com

# Praseban Resort
## ประเสบัน รีสอร์ท

**Type:** Resort
**Style:** Contemporary Thai-Balinese
**Room type:** 16 Rooms; 6 Maarataar Deluxe Rooms, 3 Sawanya Rooms,
2 Minntra Beach Front Rooms, 2 Praseban Suite Rooms,
1 Praseban Ocean Room, 2 Narin Tara Family Rooms
**Room rate:** 4,000 to 14,000 THB
**Facilities:** Pool, Restaurant, Fitness
**Architect:** Somkiat Trakulboon, Kamol  Chotesmitkul
**Interior Architect:** Kamol Chotesmitkul  **Landscape Architect:** Praphat Tiranarata

Stunning in its contemporary Thai-Balinese architectural style, Praseban Resort stands out as offering a sense of luxury, comfort and privacy meticulously surrounded by tropical gardens laid out alongside a fine white sandy beach at the southern end of Pranburi.

'Praseban' is the Indonesian word meaning 'Palace for Dynasty Visitors'. The design features are inspired by Balinese style, while also combining smooth, graceful Thai forms that give a real feeling of personality. The structural layout follows a simple curving alignment that reflects luxury and elegance.

The resort offers rooms and villas in two-storey buildings and decorated in contemporary Thai-Balinese style with wood furnishings. Each room is differently designed, though all have large private balconies and are just a few steps from the beach to ensure a memorable experience.

**Address**
173, Moo 4, Paknam Pran, Pranburi, Prachuap Khiri Khan, 77220
**T:** +66 (0) 3263 0590-1, **F:** +66 (0) 3263 0589, **E:** sales@prasebanresort.com
www.prasebanresort.com

BAYBURI
VACATION VILLAS
HUA HIN
Centara
BOUTIQUE COLLECTION

# The Bayburi Vacation Villas Hua Hin,
## Centara Boutique Collection
### เบย์บุรีวาเคชันวิลลา หัวหิน เซ็นทาราบูติกคอเลกชัน

**Type:** Boutique Resort
**Style:** Modern Boutique
**Room type:** 4 Villas; 1 Mediterranean Retreat, 1 Pacific Hideaway,
1 Modern Tropical, 1 Scandinavian Vacation
**Room rate:** 45,000 THB
**Facilities:** Pool
**Architect and Landscape Architect:** Q plus Q
**Interior Architect:** dwp

The Bayburi Villas is a complex of four privately owned luxury beachfront villas with an outstanding location in one of Thailand's least known areas. Unlike neighbouring Hua Hin, the beach at Pranburi is restful and free of crowds.

Structurally, the villas are virtually identical, but in interior design and landscaping each is different. The architectural style manages to blend traditional Asian tropical with elements of contemporary Western flair. The result is four unique villas with striking visual appeal as reflected in their names, Mediterranean Retreat, Pacific Hideaway, Modern Tropical, and Scandinavian Vacation.

With their two-storey design, the villas provide between 380 and 420 square metres of space and feature three bedrooms, three bathrooms, an entertainment-cum-function room, private swimming pool with Jacuzzi and sunbath pool, maid's room, and kitchen complete with full cooking facilities. All areas are fully furnished, including artwork, appliances and linen, and are ready as vacation home rentals for short- and long-stay guests.

**Address**
306-9, Beach Front Road, Pranburi, Prachuap Khiri Khan, 77220
**T:** +66 (0)8 1858 5939, **F:** +66 (0) 2101 1235, **E:** bvh@chr.co.th
www.centarahotelsresorts.com

# Purimuntra Resort and Spa

ภูริมันตรา รีสอร์ท แอนด์ สปา

**Type:** Boutique Resort
**Style:** Luxury Oriental
**Room type:** 19 Rooms; 7 Superior Rooms, 6 Deluxe Rooms,
1 Deluxe Beach Room, 3 Sea Villas, 1 Beach Villa, 1 Beach Suite Room
**Room rate:** start from 8,000 THB
**Facilities:** Pool, Spa, Restaurant
**Architect:** Soraphat Sirising

Purimuntra Resort and Spa is located amidst the natural landscape of Nareasuan Beach, Pranburi, where a peaceful atmosphere pervades guestrooms rooms and villas. The property is flanked by a crystal-clear turquoise sea and you awaken to the sound of soft, caressing waves. A pleasant walk along the white powdery private beach brings you to Khao Kalok, Thao-Kosa Forest Park, just 400-metre away.

Facilities such as a private Jacuzzi and outdoor bathtub provide an idyllic blend of contemporary luxury living and Oriental ease. You can also relax and rejuvenate at Muntra Spa, where you will have the chance to appreciate the well-being that comes from harmony with nature. Ultimately, you'll find Purimuntra Resort and Spa characterized by a cozy yet chic atmosphere.

**Address**
97, Moo 4, Paknam Pran, Pranburi, Prachuap Khiri Khan, 77220
**T:** +66 (0) 3263 0550, **F:** +66 (0) 3263 0550 ext.312, **E:** info@purimuntra.com
www.purimuntra.com

# La a Natu Bed & Bakery

ลา เอ นาตู เบดแอนด์เบเกอรี่

**Type:** Resort
**Style:** Modern Tropical
**Room type:** 10 Units; 4 Tropical Villages, 1 Tropical Village Family, 2 Loft Suites, 3 Tropical Cottages
**Room rate:** 4,488 to 15,888 THB
**Facilities:** Pool, Restaurant
**Architect:** Direk Senghluang
**Interior Architect:** Chittada Senghluang
**Landscape Architect:** Yuwadee Sangteanchai, Varis Sakornvimol

Wonderfully situated on a secluded beach with hills at either end, La a Natu Bed & Bakery is an environmentally concerned and palate-pleasing resort. This stylish Modern Tropical resort is not luxurious, but cozy and lovely. Amid the alluring landscape of rice fields by the sea, Thai-Lao architecture and locally inspired artworks blend with modern structures and contemporary design, offering a surprising, as well as charming, combination.

Inspired by the rural landscape, La a Natu was first conceived as 'The Green Rice Field by the Blue Sea' or 'Seaside Rice Field Resort'. The accommodation is thematically categorized into three distinctive zones: Tropical Village, Tropical Cottage and Loft Suite. All are laid out along the beach and enjoy full sea views, the sand and foam just a few steps away. With partial sea views, are four Lao Song thatched houses set in a tranquil landscape of rice terraces. Each type of accommodation features distinctive interior décor.

As a 'bed and bakery', the resort's delicious homemade cakes, afternoon tea and other desserts have continued to delight resident guests and visitors since its opening in 2008.

**Address**

234, Moo 2, Sam Roi Yot, Prachuap Khiri Khan, 77120

**T:** +66 (0) 3268 9941-3, **F:** +66 (0) 3268 9944, **E:** laanatu@gmail.com

www.laanatu.com

# Brassiere Beach
บราเซีย บีช

**Type:** Resort
**Style:** Mediterranean-Country
**Room type:** 9 Rooms; 5 Sea View Rooms, 1 Private Pool Room,
1 Cliff View Room, 2 Garden View Rooms
**Room rate:** 3,800 to 11,500 THB
**Facilities:** Pool, Restaurant
**Architect:** Suthinun Sparat  **Interior Architect:** Yingluck Charoenying

Located on a beautiful spacious private beachfront overlooking Nom Sao Island, Brassiere Beach Resort sits amid lush green vegetation next to Khao Sam Roi Yot National Park.

It's a lovely resort comprising a collection of Mediterranean-inspired cottages. Each is distinctive in design and style, while all offer luxurious comfort coupled with the privacy ensured by the cottages facing in different directions. Building materials are largely a mixture of wood and white cement, along with a sprinkling of colorful mosaic reliefs in a principal scheme of blue and white. The décor elements are simple but stylish – painted cement floors and walls, a cement bed decorated which painted tiles, vintage chandelier, antique furniture, and chiffon curtains embroidered in floral patterns.

The name of this small boutique resort derives from the nearby spirit house where fishermen bring offerings of brassieres in the belief they'll bring good luck, and the nine cottages are named after such brassiere brands as Wacoal, Triumph, Victoria's Secret, Laperla, and Nobra.

**Address**
210, Moo 5, Sam Roi Yot, Prachuap Khiri Khan, 77120
**T:** +66 (0) 3263 0555, **F:** +66 (0) 3263 0554, **E:** brassierebeach@hotmail.com
www.brassierebeach.com

# X2 Hua Hin Kui Buri

## Villas by Design, Centara Boutique Collection

ครอสทูหัวหินกุยบุรี วิลลาบายดีไซน์ เซ็นทาราบูติกคอเลกชัน

**Type:** Boutique Resort
**Style:** Modern & Tropical Residence
**Room type:** 23 Villas; 19 Private Pool Villas, 4 Private Garden Villas
**Room rate:** 15,000 to 45,000 THB
**Facilities:** Pool, Restaurant, Bar
**Architect, Interior and Landscape Architect:** Duangrit Bunnag Architect

With an 80-metre-long direct beach access, the X2 (pronounced 'cross to') resort was designed to blend with its natural surroundings and offer peaceful uninterrupted views. The existing landscape with mature trees has been carefully preserved to confirm the property's links to the nearby fishing village of Baan Bangkao, Kuiburi, where nature preservation is an innate way of life. Thus a large, revered tamarind tree has become part of the welcome provided by the lobby, while other areas have similarly been laid out around the trees.

The rooms are designed so that privacy is created between each unit and intimacy within each room. The longitudinal façade of the rooms is a solid stonewall that instills a sublime visual effect as seen from the restaurant. In interior design, an 'inside out' approach has been followed. The external stonewall finishing continues inside so that the blurred threshold, from outside to inside, is strengthened, while the choice of stone delivers a profound visual coherence of buildings and nature. Natural light seeping through the ceiling openings gives dominance to the texture of the stone.

In a way, X2 is an effort to humanize the artificiality of architecture and modernism articulation, and invites guests to cross to (X2) a whole new dimension of designed luxury and experience life as it should be.

**Address**

52, Moo 13, Ao Noi, Muang, Prachuap Khiri Khan, 77210

**T:** +66 (0) 3260 1412, **F:** +66 (0) 3260 3429, **E:** x2kb@chr.co.th

www.centarahotelsresorts.com

Boutique villa by the sea...
**NishaVille**
Resort & Spa

# Nisha Ville Resort and Spa

ณิชาวิลล์ รีสอร์ท แอนด์ สปา

**Type:** Boutique Villa Resort

**Style:** Seaside Cottage

**Room type:** 36 Villas; 2 Breeze Villas, 4 Sea Villas, 24 Sand Villas, 6 Canal Villas

**Room rate:** 8,000 to 27,000 THB

**Facilities:** Pool, Spa, Restaurant, Lounge, Bar, Fitness

**Architect:** Pandarat Indraphim

**Interior and Landscape Architect:** Weerachart Teerachartphat c/o KIJ Development

Nisha Ville's harmonious design and casual tropical architecture merge seamlessly with the natural surroundings, luxuriant with indigenous plants and trees. The resort nestles in the picturesque fishing village of Huay Yang, as yet undiscovered by the tourist crowds, and is set beside a pristine beach, a secret haven of peace and serenity.

Located next to the beach, the villas are designed in a fresh and vibrant style with open-plan interiors and shady terraces. Light and airy, they are perfectly suited for casual tropical living. The 36 seaside cottages are set in 27 acres of landscaped tropical gardens, allowing superb views of the unspoiled beach or out over a tranquil freshwater canal that meanders through the property. Each villa features a large outdoor terrace, open-plan living and dining areas, luxurious bedrooms and spacious 'designer' bathrooms with separate bathtub and shower.

Fully equipped European-style kitchens include coffee and tea making facilities, a microwave, dishwasher, and a clothes washer and dryer, making the villas perfect for both short-stay and long-stay guests.

**Address**

333, Moo 7, Baan Huay Yang, Huay Yang, Thap Sakae, Prachuap Khiri Khan, 77130

**T:** +66 (0) 2508 5335, **F:** +66 (0) 2508 5335, **E:** rsvn@nishavilleresort.com

www.nishavilleresort.com

**Editor-in-Chief**
Nithi Sthapitanonda
**Managing Editor**
Suluck Visavapattamawon
**Editor**
Pisut Lertdumrikarn
**Project Coordinator**
Bussara Keamapirak

**English Text Editor**
Anthony John Hoskin
**Translator (Introduction)**
Jutamas Tadthiemrom

**Graphic Designer**
Vatanya Bongkotkarn

**Sketch**
Sasi Veerasethakul
**Map Illustrator**
Paloch Lilittham

**Photographer**
Beer Singnoi
**Contributing Photographer**
Krisada Boonchaleow, Pisut Lertdumrikarn,
Pruk Dejkhamhaeng, Thitiwoot Chaisawataree,
Vatanya Bongkotkarn, Wison Tungthunya,
Spaceshift Studio, Trip Magazine

**Sponsor Coordinator**
Pimpattra Kosalanun

**Photography Credit**

t = Top, b = Bottom, l = Left, r = Right, c = Center

**Beer Singnoi:** 5l-c, 9tl, 278bl, 279cr, Back Cover t, br, Cher Resort: 16-17, 21t, 21br \
Devasom Hua Hin Resort: 31, 33br, 34, 35b, 36b, 37tc-r, 37b \
The Herb by the Sea Hotel and Spa: 67tr, 67bl-c \
Dune Hua Hin Hotel: 70, 73bl \ The Hen Hua Hin: 78t, 79t, 79bl, 81t \
Baan Bayan Beach Hotel: 96-97, 98t, 100, 101t, 101bl \
The Lapa Hua Hin: 119, 122t, 125bl \ Hua Him Mantra Resort: 152r \
Supatra Hua Hin Resort: 170 \ Riad Hua Hin: 181 \
The Bihai Hua Hin: 187, 188t, 188bl, 189bl \ Pran-A-Luxe: 197tl \
Foresta Resort Pranburi: 211, 213bc \ Ali Baba Resort Pranburi: 215-216, 217b, 219bl \
Aleenta Resort & Spa: 221-222, 223tl, 223b, 224t, 225t, 226, 227t, 227bl \
Praseban Resort: 230, 232, 233t, 233br, 234tr, 234b, 235tc \
Purimuntra Resort and Spa: 249tl \ La a Natu Bed & Bakery: 253, 255-256, 257t, 257bl-c
**Krisada Boonchaleow:** End Paper, 10-11, 4l, 44-45, 5r, 8t, 8cl, 8bc-r, 9tr, 9cc, 9b, 153t, 155b, 190-191, 278bl, 278cr, 278br, 279tl, 279tr, 279b
**Pisut Lertdumrikarn:** 213br, 257br
**Praphat Tiranarata:** 235t, 235br
**Pruk Dejkhamhaeng:** 57, 59b, 63t, 63bl
**Thitiwoot Chaisawataree:** 9cr, 97bl, 97br, 99t, 99bl
**Vatanya Bongkotkarn:** 114-115, 219br, 277br
**Wison Tungthunya:** 265, 267, 269br
**Openbox:** 62, 63bc
**Spaceshift Studio:** 175-179
**Trip Magazine:** 188br, 189t, 189bc

All other photos courtesy of listed hotels.

**Special thanks to the following individuals and companies**
Ploy Chariyaves, Dr. Yuwarat Hemasilpin
BAB, Duangrit Bunnag Architect, mooof, Openbox, The Office of Bangkok Architect (OBA), Trend Design, Cher Resort, Aleenta Resort & Spa, Hua Hin – Pranburi

# BAYBURI VACATION VILLAS HUA HIN, CENTARA BOUTIQUE COLLECTION

## BAYBURI
VACATION VILLAS
HUA HIN

*As Individual as You*

BOUTIQUE COLLECTION

A range of vacation villas for a new kind of exclusive holiday experience where atmosphere is intimate and style is individual.

Themed Bayburi Vacation Villas are situated on the pristine beach of Pranburi and each self-contained unit enjoys a spacious living space with three bedrooms, three bathrooms and its own private swimming pool.

Whether you seek a comfortable family holiday or quality time with your friends, you will find it at the Bayburi Vacation Villas Hua Hin. Make yourself at home.

306-9 Beach Front Road, Pak Nam Pran, Pranburi, Prachuab Khirikhan 77220, Thailand
T +66 (0)8 2769 1234   E bvh@chr.co.th   www.centara.co.th/bvh

The greatest gift is to give unceasingly.

SINGHA CORPORATION Co., Ltd.

*Breathtaking, challenging, awe-inspiring, amazing.*

There are parts of Thailand that haven't changed in thousands of years. What is truly amazing is being able to explore such beautiful places without affecting the environment. Whether it's treks through mountainous hilltribe villages or trips through mangrove forests, you will be truly amazed at our diverse landscape. Whether you are planning the trip of a lifetime or you are a regular visitor to Thailand, one thing that's certain is you will always be amazed.

amazing
**THAILAND**
*Always Amazes You*
www.tourismthailand.org